WASHING WINDOWS TOO

Irish Women Write Poetry

Alan Hayes and Nuala O'Connor

editors

ARLEN
HOUSE

WASHING WINDOWS TOO
Irish Women Write Poetry

is published in 2022 by
ARLEN HOUSE
42 Grange Abbey Road
Baldoyle
Dublin D13 A0F3, Ireland
arlenhouse@gmail.com
arlenhouse.ie

978–1–85132–311–1, *paperback*

Distributed internationally by
SYRACUSE UNIVERSITY PRESS
621 Skytop Road, Suite 110
Syracuse
New York
13244–5290
supress@syr.edu
syracuseuniversitypress.syr.edu

Typesetting by Arlen House

cover image: 'Figures' by Mainie Jellett
watercolour and gouache, 39 x 26 cm

ARTS COUNCIL of Northern Ireland

LOTTERY FUNDED

CONTENTS

Visual Poems

Eavan Boland, 1986

In 1984, Catherine Rose, Arlen House's publisher, and editor Eavan Boland, founded Women's Education Bureau (WEB) to develop workshops, mentorship and supportive creative spaces for women.

Eavan Boland travelled Ireland hosting workshops and encouraging women. At one event a writer told Eavan she was reluctant to 'go public'. She said she couldn't tell her neighbours she was a poet – because they would think she didn't wash her windows.

Preface
POETRY, POWER AND PRIVILEGE

Alan Hayes

These 100 new poems which comprise *Washing Windows Too* give us great hope for the future of Irish poetry. I invited 150 women, who have yet to publish a full poetry collection, to submit unpublished poems for consideration, and from over 500 poems received I made this selection. There were difficult choices to make – the poetic talent out there is immense.

Here are the voices who will shape a new poetry world. These writers come from all parts of the island and beyond. The age range spans over seven decades, and, as with all Arlen House anthologies, diversity is integrated throughout, in all its glory and in all its honesty. This anthology is representative of a new society and a new way of accepting and honouring the talent all around us.

Though it has not always been so.

Women who are poets have not always been accepted or welcomed on equal terms. Talent has not always been the key factor. Power structures operate in dark corners.

There were better times. The nineteenth century was a golden time for Irish women writers, relatively speaking. Anne Colman, in truly groundbreaking research in pre-internet days, discovered over 700 women writing poetry during the 1800s. In current research I'm undertaking, I have discovered dozens of Irish women publishing poetry collections in the early decades of the twentieth century. However, from the 1950s onwards, conservative powerbrokers chose to champion their male peers, and in most instances female voices were silenced. I believe there were always female voices around who could be silenced.

Galway, 1975: Arlen House – Ireland's pioneering first feminist press – was established by Catherine Rose. She gathered together a small group of other extraordinary women, including young poet Eavan Boland, who brought visionary ideas and practical help, and feminist activist and seer, Dr Margaret Mac Curtain, who was one of the leading voices campaigning for equality in society. I believe all women writing today owe a debt of gratitude to these women who were the first to open doors, at a time when it was difficult and dangerous to do so. These women started a new creative movement, demanding a space and a voice and a vision for women writers. Thus commenced a new flowering, which we continue to witness today.

Though it may not always be so.

Unless systemic changes are made and enforced, progressive improvements in equality and diversity can always be dismantled. Power systems operate by twisted untruths.

I was delighted to invite Nuala O'Connor to co-edit *Washing Windows Too*. In her stunning introduction she reflects on the power and importance of poetry and considers many of the fascinating themes emerging in this anthology. In 2002, Nuala submitted the manuscript of her first collection to Arlen House. We were thus privileged to introduce one of the most original and important voices of the twenty-first century. In 2002, the poetry world was vastly different to today. It was a space that was not as open and welcoming to women. I remember one young female poet saying she was told, rather patronisingly and condescendingly, that there was not one line of poetry in her manuscript – an opinion that awards judges, media reviewers and a large audience utterly disagreed with.

Diversity was not even a buzzword in the artistic lexicon then, despite the fact that equality legislation had recently been enacted, and equality and diversity measures should have been implemented by all powerbrokers and decision-makers – it is inexplicable why it has taken so long, and disturbing when it is done so ineptly at times now. Often, Jessie Lendennie at Salmon Poetry remained a lone beacon advocating progress and change in the poetry world. And sometimes a price had to be paid for doing so. Powerful publishers in the western world continued their long-standing exclusionary practices, often with the public support and approval of funding bodies; in Ireland the output of poetry presses, generally, was not reflective of modern society.

But the growing body of women poets, many of whom emerged from Arlen House/Eavan Boland's pioneering WEB workshops, demanded opportunities; they refused to be silenced or sidelined. Thus, a new beginning for poetry in both the English and Irish languages.

With the right supports, independent management, and honest engagement by the entire arts world, this is the perfect time to create opportunities for growth and blossoming.

Power structures remain stubbornly resistant to real change. We are told 'change takes time' – though nobody explains why that is so. And why do *we* allow it to be so?

Over recent decades, the Irish poetry world has become increasingly younger, female and more diverse; a fact not represented adequately by powerbrokers and decision-makers. Indeed, the alliteration in my title, 'Poetry, Power and Privilege', gently teased me to add another representative 'P' word – with 'Pricks' being an obvious option – but I choose to refrain, for now.

In *Washing Windows Too*, there are strong familial and community ties: three of the poets are daughters of famous writers, Molly Keane, Eithne Strong and Angela Greene; there are mother and daughter poets. Many of the women have contributed to Ireland's cultural life for many decades as prose writers. Two are famous visual artists. All have an interest in poetry, often from the days when an interest was not encouraged or welcomed. I put on the record that there were so many other voices we couldn't include, who deserve to be included. Though a volume 3 of *Washing Windows* is already in our vision ...

For recommendations, advice and wisdom, we thank Geraldine Mills, Phyl Herbert, Nessa O'Mahony, Donal Ryan, Luke Morgan, Celia de Fréine, Maureen Boyle, Joseph Woods, Eileen Casey, Lynda Tavakoli and Joseph O'Connor.

For now, let us raise our voices to celebrate these 100 new poets, help them on their journeys and watch as they bring new vitality into Irish and international creative life.

And let it always be so.

Introduction
A VOICE ANSWERING A VOICE

Nuala O'Connor

'... let the soft animal of your body/love what it loves' Mary Oliver wrote in her poem 'Wild Geese', and what a pleasure it is for a reader to see what subjects new poets love enough – feel urgently enough about – to be moved to create poetry. The writers in the pages of *Washing Windows Too* have things on their minds that have exploded into that love-urgency that makes writers write. And, just as it should be, few subjects are off limits. A poet may not always love her inspirational material, but those here revere the act of writing so much – value it so much – that honing their ideas, visions, and insights into poem-shaped, concrete objects has become crucial. It is an honour to witness what has urged these writers to the process of thought, cogitation, sentence, and finally, poem.

Many writers use writing as an attempt to solve life's conundrums – to solve themselves. And to understand the self and others better, too, because writing is the best way they know to gain sight into, and survive, the vagaries of life. For me, this process of moulding words and ideas into lasting shape is tied into my well-being – I write in order to make peace with things, to figure them out, or to honour certain moments. I write because, if I didn't, I think I would lose my mind. Perhaps the writers in this anthology are like me – maybe for them, too, writing is their sanity and their joy, their best thinking and settling tool. A poem can be a path into the deepest, purest self, and back out again – through the very act of writing – to a calmer, less frenetic place.

Creative acts rarely happen in a vacuum. Poets write alone, but in chorus with other writers, and with the world. In her novel *Orlando* Virginia Woolf wrote, 'Was not writing poetry a secret transaction, a voice answering a voice?' The women in this anthology know those transactional bargains, they write with their foremother poets whispering in their ears, they are alert to their voices and they, in turn, want to whisper in other ears. Orla Fay in her poem 'The Reader Finds the Writer Lost in the Woods' is outside the poem, as a reader, but she is, too, a 'follower of the trail./A thought on the river./A shifting of energy, an idea ordained.' Fay, and all of these poets, write in the knowledge that other women – their daughters, their younger friends – will deal with similar, familiar issues to theirs, and may be moved to dig deep and write about them too. And these writers also understand that their sister-poets will have to deal with as yet undreamed-of problems and joys. The writers here use their knowledge and their voices to chime with their kin-poets and other women, to offer comfort and illumination.

Because poets deal with issues that concern them – universal truths, often – certain themes emerge, as they do in all anthologies. In *Washing Windows Too*, particular groupings of motifs re-occur and these include birth and motherhood; child-love and empty nests; migration and refugees; women's power and agency; bodies, the male gaze, and violence; nature and its beauties; art, creation, and the act of writing itself; uneasy relationships; politics; health and illness; and grief and death. And, because we are living in the early twenty-twenties, the pandemic naturally features in some poems.

Love, where it is overtly mentioned, is often tricky and circumspect, but sometimes it bursts into joy, as in Jacqui Burgess's blow-in poem 'I Blew in on a Tide of Love' where she writes '... the heart has its reasons/for unswerving devotion./Only that the heart of the world sings/in the stones of memory,/whispering her secrets in wild places,/ deep in love.' Other poets are searching for love; Anesu Khanya Mtowa writes 'I can't stop writing poems for the lover I have never met', but says when she meets her, she will, generously, 'not stop to write a thing. I will leave her be/to breathe/from beyond the page/... And if she asks, I will let her burn every word/I ever made her out to be.'

Mothers feature strongly, as is to be expected in an all-woman anthology. 'In Sepia' by Doreen Duffy is a tight, devastatingly affecting lyric about a mother who does not want to be a parent: 'silence filled her, day after day'. Orlagh O'Farrell also acknowledges that mothers can contain multitudes, and shines her light on another tricky mother in 'On the Side of the Volcano': 'You've been a bright slope, mother,/one of those bright dangerous slopes/where magma's never far from surfacing.'

Mothers are naturally present in poems about childbirth, but some writers refuse to make a uniformly beatific moment of birth, rather they examine the sometimes harsh, sometimes joyful experiences women really have. 'Bearing Witness' by Jean James is in the form of a celebratory letter to a daughter who is labouring to deliver her own daughter, in a birthing pool: 'she stays, anchored to her cord/until the next wave crashes,/launching her up and out, onto your mothership.'

By contrast, Jackie Lynam writes starkly of the vulnerability of a woman in childbirth in 'Silenced':

I'm naked from the waist down
when they arrive;
a cavalry of white coats,
baby-faced, blank stares.

Incapable of summoning words,
my tongue ripped out by medical artillery
– it's been thirty hours since my waters broke.

Creativity, and the act of creation, is pleasingly present in the anthology and is explored in poems like Kate Arthur's 'October, Towards Archie's Bridge'. She writes: 'sometimes it helps the work to have discomfort/ sometimes we work better with constraints' – a feeling every writer surely knows.

In her clever poem 'What to Expect When You're Punctuating', Helena Nolan doubles up on creativity, combining the title of a pregnancy manual with the act of writing: 'Now/say that the lives of children/are the lines of poems you are writing/on a womb-white page.'

Alice Kinsella in 'Sylvia Plath is Sitting in my Father's Chair' has a conversation on the right to write whatever moves her, with sister-writer Plath: 'Are you going to write today,/about something other than the dead?' Plath asks. 'Fuck off,' is the poet's succinct reply. She watches Plath leave: 'It's miles from my house to the road./She leaves barefoot, and I do not follow.'

American-Irish poet Jennifer Matthews examines problems of harassment and silencing in the literary world, in her powerful, *cri de coeur* poem, 'Selkie':

You like to dance in the moonlight, barelegged.
You like to take stories into your body and rebirth them.
You like to press words into the pleasure of puzzles.
There's no dance unless Selkie slips out of her skin.
There is no performance without an audience to listen.
There's no collection without a spine & a recommendation.

Ava Ní Loinsigh concludes that the answers to life's conundrums may not always lie in writing poetry. In 'Uaireanta Níl Filíocht Oiriúnach' she tells us 'Running around trying to record everything,/is to recall, pen in our hands,/there is something nice about looking back ...'. She writes: 'uaireanta bíonn sé níos fearr gan scríobh/faoi roinnt rudaí fiú dá mbeadh ort an fonn.'

Sarah Strong considers what the lifeblood nature of writing meant to her author-mother Eithne Strong, who continued to write, despite debilitating pain: 'The doctor said her/rotator cuff muscles were lax,/taxed as she was with babies,/breast-feeding/and writing her poems.'

Two writers – Susan Knight and Ellie Rose McKee – approach writing with welcome humour. In 'After the Reading', Knight considers the phenomenon of shortcut writers, those who want experienced authors to fast-track them to the prize – publication:

> He fixes me with a lugubrious eye. I'm a softie
> and anyway no one else is talking to me right now.
> What is it? I ask. Fifty thousand words, he says.
> I suspect they're all in that large brown envelope
> clutched under his arm.
> One word and he'll hand it over.
> I say nothing.

McKee ruminates on procrastination, a flush of ideas, and the need to create *something*, in 'Is it Problematic to Think My Muse May Have ADHD?' She says 'I pick up a pen/and my fingers itch for a paintbrush' but, while busily distracted, she ends up inevitably picking up her pen again.

Politics is examined in several poems, overtly by Shauna Gilligan in '1922' a tight, beautiful poem of betrayal, and by Yvonne Boyle in an elegy for murdered journalist Lyra McKee. Anita Gracey and Rosemary Jenkinson also write about the Troubles in Northern Ireland. Gracey sets 'The Runt of the Litter' in the early years of the 1970s: 'I was more rage than girl/as the streets squealed fire'. Rosemary Jenkinson, in 'Sandy Row Riots', uses visceral language to centre the reader in the confusion and horror of constant unrest:

Enfurnaced people, copter-crazy,
entranced by gauzy wraiths
from flaming underbellies of engines
that catch like fireweed,
come from the east and Tiger's Bay.

Politics, feminism, food, and power find a perfect mix in Breda Spaight's lively 'Mother's Plum Pudding':

Mix one pound each of jail-bait raisins
and #MeToo currants with finely chopped
patriarchy suet. Add a half teaspoon of
pornography nutmeg, two of pope's penis
allspice; one of glass ceiling cinnamon;
one cup of candied faking it, followed by
the grated rind of one ball-buster lemon.

Also on the theme of empowerment, 'Riding the Tiger' by Mim Greene uses anger as a positive force, in a poem about women rising up to claim their space: 'No shame,/no shame. No more,/no more, I will let my anger roar.'

Nithy Kasa turns to her Congolese origins and the reclaiming of tradition for powerful purposes: 'waist beads, how men love/these things around women./But we bought our beads for ourselves'. Ruth Quinlan, too, explores sexual power and confidence in 'The Life of a Scholar' with fingernails that 'were eagle talons, electric blue or poppy red,/grown to scratch my name in ogham on the line of a spine.'

June Caldwell's potent prose poem 'Predator Fuck' lays out the phenomenon of the bullied boy who turns into a bully-predator:

I'm trying very hard to show concern, to explain his
behaviour ten years on, when, in the classroom, park, or

office, or down by the canal, how he chooses who to take it out on, who's to pay for those tactless things we all go through, take on young, digest, deal with, here he lets me down, the sly predator fuck. He's completely polite, charming even, approaching whoever, asking them out. Gets hitched, she doesn't even notice the jiggy leg in the pub when he glares at other women, the inappropriate things he says, over and over, laughing it off, the times he doesn't return home ...

The suppression of women's importance is tackled in two poems featuring women related to Oscar Wilde, one being the historic narrative 'Hallowe'en Ball' by Katie Martin, which looks at the horrendous killing by accidental burning of two of Wilde's sisters, Emily and Mary, and the cover-up of their deaths. Martin writes:

Rolled in the snow, too late,
the ugly sisters now. They suffered
on for days. The record states
'Wylie' was their name.

The in-between nature of refugees and immigrants is covered in several strong poems, including Mairéad Donnellan's affecting 'The Syrian Violin Maker' where she looks at 'the slow sawing of a life divided'. Denise Nagle, in the heartrending 'How to Disappear', looks at the displacement of Syrian people:

After an explosion
you wear your powdered past.
Silence is your new parlance.

Lani O'Hanlon brings the pandemic to the fore in her moving 'In the Time of No Touch', detailing a practical, poignant solution to help the dying where 'nurses filled plastic gloves with warm water,/placed one over and one under the dying person's hand,/to mimic the pressure, the warmth/of a living hand – the hand of God they called it.'

Saakshi Patel in 'Bashiran' takes an unusual look at optimism and heart, in the light of one woman's thankless work, and the men she supports by her labour. This woman 'sings her way through washing clothes' for other people and 'her purse jingles' by night. However, the poem continues:

[it] empties out as cheap illicit spirit
into her husband's liver, turning him brusque,
fuelling his habit, enraging mind and fist.
She saves remaining change for her son's bail,
prances to work, refills her purse the next day.

Nature is celebrated in several poems, but Eilis Stanley comes at it slant, writing about cyberspace dominance, and the refusal by some to be in the now, and to admire the natural world, in 'A Grumble from Gaia', where she is 'grieving the vanished act of looking':

... a bereft sky won't bother changing
hues anymore; depressed cumuli huddle in waiting
rooms and windless tunnels.

The world has known too much grief in the last couple of years and these writers want to explore it. The anthology opens on Sonia Abercrombie's sharp, lovely elegy for Molly whose parlour was 'dressed in the buttermilk of dowry linen' – the poem mourns not just a woman who lives on in the natural world she revered, but also the passing of a particular collective, rural way of life. Other elegies include a lament for recently murdered Irish woman Ashling Murphy, by Helen McClements, who writes 'I wonder if she knows that we hold her close'.

Catherine McCabe, in 'Orca Mother', offers a beautiful and universal poem about death:

And isn't grief strange?
The way realisation of loss weighs heavier
than the dead carcass of a little one,
so loved.

Sarah O'Connor skilfully combines pregnancy loss and writing in her 'Airplane Lullaby', where she says, 'my little love, you were the single stanza/I had housed for us both/oh, how we had wanted/all your poetry to bloom'.

Micheline Egan takes a softer look at death in her sweetly irreverent 'Passing Through', where the narrator has thoughtfully stocked a beloved's coffin with the *RTÉ Guide* and posh chocolates.

The writer bell hooks said that 'the function of art is to do more than tell it like it is – it's to imagine what is possible.' Each poet in *Washing Windows Too* has taken the inkwell of imagination, and all of its possibilities, and allowed it to spill over through love, anger, appreciation, reason, grief, and opinion onto these pages. The voices in this anthology whisper their secrets and rise together in harmony on an ink-tide of word-love and humanity. For these poets, may it always be possible for them to do just that, and for us to listen.

WASHING WINDOWS TOO

Sonia Abercrombie

HER HOUSE

Molly's house has been without a light these three years.
She's like the African Violet I brought to her
knowing well it could fade in the shade of her rooms.
First, her geese were sold, then her weekly visits dwindled,
herself alone with the open door, the pot on the fire,
a rustle of mice around the edge of her kitchen,
the sun straining in through green glass and geranium.
Suddenly, the place darkened,
as if silence were a person renting.
Abandoned, her cats went wild,
even the crows ceased coming.
Her roses' stretched stems grew as fast as hawthorn.
No gossip or chuckles, tomato sandwiches
or a slip of whiskey,
an exchange of news or each other's histories.

I imagine her parlour this day,
now knitted with dust, in cobwebs.
I glimpsed it only once on a gentle afternoon.
It was dressed in the buttermilk of dowry linen.
The river is her echo, pines her aged, knotted hands,
her hair like a bushel of hay left by a farmer in winter.
I breathe the pulse of the river now
as it chants past the primrose banks,
over-spills the rushy land in the wild months.
Yesterday, her nephew crossed the fields like a poacher.
He has cut her roses down. She watches over her house
and her lamb-less fields as the moon in the trap of trees.

Síle Agnew

JOY

Every day a woman is emerging,
transforming the little girl
who once sat on my lap.

Your smile as you walk out the door,
on the way to a party
you will be the soul of.

Your tireless campaign
to repeal laws and gift women
with choice instead of shame.

After the drought of not seeing you,
the warm hug of your texts
brings you here in a moment,

like droplets of rain on
parched petals of parenthood,
until our conversations match in time.

You bring joy,
find joy,
leave joy in your wake.

Kate Arthur

OCTOBER, TOWARDS ARCHIE'S BRIDGE

A preference for this time of dying,
when we can see the bare bones
start to show. Often my mind is too crowded to think
in straight lines.
The hedgerow is grey,
a plume of smoke rising up inside it,

the flame long since put out.
You work at it with a drypoint needle on acetate.
You say sometimes it helps the work to have discomfort;
sometimes we work better with constraints.

The black soil with the base notes.
We made a blank sheet of it and cut out our own frame.
Held it away to let the light pass through.

Trish Bennett

A MAN'S WORLD

In the nineties
I was an engineer,
new to the job
and keen to impress.

When I was told to entertain
our new customer
from the Middle East

I took him out
for a bite of lunch
and a walk by the lake
to stretch the legs.

He invited me to work
for his company, said
*You'll earn ten times
what you make here*

*but in my country,
the women walk
two steps behind
the men.*

I politely declined his offer,
and for the rest of his visit
kept one step ahead.

Clodagh Beresford Dunne

CHOCOLATE ADVENT CALENDAR
for William

The 1st of December.

Your four year old thumb
aimed at Window *One*
of your Spiderman Advent Calendar.

It takes a surgeon's concentration
to bite your lower lip and make that incision
into pre-breakfast-chocolate heaven.

A Christmas star
you place on your tongue, like a soluble cure,
allow it to melt into you, merge with you,
become one.

In the milieu of the school run
it goes unnoticed that you've turned all *Carpe Diem*
and seized the opportunity to unseal
windows 2, 3, 4, 5, 6 and 7.

At your desk, you wait for the day to tick away.
Wisdom, understanding, fortitude
fly over your head like a white dove.

And so, by nightfall, you prove
that, beyond all laws of time,
24 days can be rolled into 1.

Yvonne Boyle

TRIBUTE TO LYRA MCKEE

You wrote about
the intended harm and
unintended suffering of those years.
Your mind cleared
of our post agreement fears.
Your talent a bright star.
Some 'do not regret their stance,'
some 'try to steer others on another path'
and others, including those younger than the voting age,
still fuel dissonance and death.

You were a fresh witness to that wanton rage.
Dark night   disturbance   fear   adrenalin.
Your partner looks around
and finds you on the ground
and then will never find you, as you were,
again.

And we, weary in the knowledge of
the old embedded sights and sounds of violence,
ask what can writers say now?
Ricochet raw,
another red and precious scar,
haphazard horror.
You were not afraid
to enter the echo chamber of loss,
your spirit sucked through
a terrible aperture,
                resonating
                resounding
                astounding.

Caroline Bracken

THE CYAN ROUTE

You lost your mind
somewhere on the N11
when we were driving
from Dublin to Wexford.
It flew out the car window
along with joy
on a day in September or November
one of those ember months
when it was cool but still
warm enough to roll
the windows down
just enough to keep
our breath clean.
I should have insisted
on closing them
switched to aircon
kept you both safe.
I think it happened
on the Cyan Route
near the ringfort
and the Lost Village of the Downs.
I have driven that road
over and over since then
searching for signs in the gorse verges
beyond the cat's eyes under bridges
in the branches of rowan
and ash. I change speed
swop lanes
go at daybreak and midnight
in sunlight or snow.
No matter the temperature
I keep the windows closed
tight.

Clodagh Brennan Harvey

THE BATTLE OF GABHRA
after Ella Young

Fionn was led into the room of old warriors;
his eyes adjusting to the gloom,
he recognized them, one by one –
    still proud, manly,
        even in their frail dotage.

How was Fionn to know
it was only Oisín and Caoilte would survive,
living on into the time of Patrick;
that the massive build of these two
was a source of wonder
to the men of God who
ministered to their needs –
    gathering round them,
        listening in awe,
        writing down the tales of Fionn and the fianna
        that we might have them still.

Jacquie Burgess

I BLEW IN ON A TIDE OF LOVE

I blew in on a tide of love,
no intention to fall so deep
into this land of water and stones,
of saints, scholars, radiant sinners,
or know the shame and confusion
of colonial ancestors.

I dance on the bones,
on endless layers of lives long gone.
Fierce flames, scurrying wild creatures,
bone weary earth dwellers.
Do they rest in peace or roar for justice?
Begging a cup of kindness for pity's sake.

What can I possibly know,
blown in by accident or strange design?
Only that the heart has its reasons
for unswerving devotion.
Only that the heart of the world sings
in the stones of memory,
whispering her secrets in wild places,
deep in love.

June Caldwell

PREDATOR FUCK

Poem about predator fuck as young boy, wearing an
argyle jumper, loves UFOs, mandarin oranges in his silky
hands, running from souped-up Da who smells of whiskey
farts, gripping a piece of string, taunting him, enjoying it.
Ma's there too, doing level best, stirring gravy, she says
pulling teeth won't take long, over in a jiffy, pain will
vamoose for best little goose. Da ties string to predator
fuck's tooth, knots the rest around doorhandle, pulls. 'This
is how it's done boyo!' Brother claps, sister sidles in with
wry green eye, sneers, 'Your turn to whinge like a wibbly
bitch!' Barbara two doors down is very kind: but predator
fuck fucks up when lured, 'Terry Tortoise will cheer you
up!' she says. He yanks her hair, smacks, kicks. I'm raging
with the little predator fuck, I wanted to try due reason,
gradually, protracted time, layers of complexity, a past
painted in the usual numbers, bullied at school, crap at
sports, empty. Darts thrown at the back of his legs,
horselaughs from lads dishing out awful humiliations,
flinging him into puddles. I wanted to show him pissing
his pants, anticipation of knife-edge fear, retching, how he
had to keep running to and from, loneliness so vast it
weeds around him, how they keep calling him a fucktwat,
gobshite, abomination, girls say so too, say he's got greasy
skin, stares a lot. Girls are bitches, girls are cunts, girls ...
I'm trying very hard to show concern, to explain his
behaviour ten years on, when, in the classroom, park, or
office, or down by the canal, how he chooses who to take it
out on, who's to pay for those tactless things we all go
through, take on young, digest, deal with, here he lets me
down, the sly predator fuck. He's completely polite,
charming even, approaching whoever, asking them out.
Gets hitched, she doesn't even notice the jiggy leg in the

pub when he glares at other women, the inappropriate things he says, over and over, laughing it off, the times he doesn't return home, or when he does he's angry, seething, the Universe owes him a thousand whores, all of that, and no matter how much it's only a matter of time before cops knock and he says, with trademark calm: 'I raped a girl last night', it doesn't happen. No, nothing happens, he's doing grand. Out for a stroll on his tod in the dark without so much as looking behind him. And he's smiling, he is, the predator fuck, boy from long ago rushing to keep up.

Barbara not too far off in front either.

Mary Rose Callaghan

L PLATES

If you type, you can drive, I'm told.
But there's one important difference.
A computer doesn't move,
not in my experience.
L plates on and I'm off aged 70.
'They're for my youngest,' I lie to the Ban Garda.
I can't turn right, so stick to circuitous left.
Going one way round the world,
I fail the test without a killing.
But it's not the open prairie,
I only need to get home safe.
No worries re Red Cow roundabouts,
or crying down the years on hard shoulders.
By night headlights show the ditches.
The road is where the darkness is.

Louise G. Cole

CAVE PAINTINGS IN THE DORDOGNE

It's an august path to thumb-print animals,
deep-etched in ochre and crushed wood-ash,
aligned along mountain walls, in caves
weather-carved into dwellings, where once
we lived, loved, learned to leave a lasting mark.

Shamans pranced, danced among pebbles,
stoned, painted dreams upon the walls,
picked at the seams of heaven's dark cloth,
silver-stitched with threads from then,
to when the future spilled into the past.

Now, we find these hidden images of bison,
bears and deer, see stick-men lying prostrate,
tangled locks combed over in iron oxide.
But they're unready for our poisoned chalice,
modern mould blooming over their ancient art.

Martina Dalton

AFTERMATH

It took too much away.
Even my favourite birds.
A broken sea wall and a painted hut

where someone used to write.
Sandhills had seen the worst of it;
from my bed I'd seen the dunes catch fire,

knew how fragile grasses are.
Thought their very roots would go.
I dreaded telling you about it.

Nothing left of it now
but the rubble scars in mud
and a broken sea wall I think I'll include

as a reminder of what was done,
and a greater wall built from what was left.
All the debris of my youth

packed solid – with topsoil
containing rare orchids.
And some rubbish from the fishing boats.

A marsh that looks like a Petri dish –
reeds in rounded culture-clumps,
agar as the sea.

Everything calm and wet,
smoothed over with a pallet knife.
And the wounded scars,

a place to fill at night – with birds.

Olga Dermott-Bond

ON FINDING OUT TOO LATE THAT MY MUM HAS
(CANCER) BECAUSE (SHE KEPT IT A SECRET)

I don't even know what hospital she means.
Pre-op this Friday. I can only guess
what the consultant looks like, a screen
beside his desk, an examination to press
where it hurts. Here. My identity band
of *sometimes daughter* will hang too loose, name
blurred. I dream of the kitchen clock's hidden hands,
her return to flowerpots shivering their shamed
faces. Will she put the kettle on, to drown
out the silence? Black tea. My day will stay
as normal, I suppose, her surgical gown
awkward under my dress, so far away

as they remove an undisclosed amount
of my mother's flesh. Our cells too many to count.

Sorcha de Brún

AN DUFAIR

Cuireann an Rí air a mhasc:
'In aimsir seo na paindéime
caithfear a bheith aireach'.

Tugann siad bualadh bos dó:
In amharclann an tsaoil,
is é atá buacach.

Cultúr is inchreidteacht
culaith na sibhialtachta:
Iad ag faire go cúramach.

Ar mhachaire parthais
clúdaíonn masc na cúirtéise
a lucht leanúna agus an fimíneach.

Má tá creideamh ag an Rí
is ann féin a chreideann,
agus sin go caolchúiseach.

Má tá teanga ar bith ag an Saoi
clúdaíonn an masc a uaillmhianta
iad ráite go fuarchúiseach.

Tá an masc caite is an claíomh sáite:
Dá áille an machaire
titeann gach dufair
go talamh go foréigneach
in am is i dtrátha —

Deirdre Devally

DOES MY BUM LOOK BIG IN THIS?

Should I be offended if he casts
an eye on my bum,
or offended if he doesn't?

My young womanhood happened
in the twilight zone
of the end of the era of the dreaded girdle
(elasticated daughter to the cruel corset,
a Guantanamo-worthy implement of torture)
and the blessed invention of body-shapers,
breath sucking crab-claws
morphing into silken caressers.
Always – drawers in of unwanted,
often imagined flesh.

Dependence on what God gave us
was of great concern
to women in my mother's day,
and in my day and my grand-daughter's day,
it seems into eternity.

So, tell me, I promise I won't be upset.
Does my bum look big in this?

Mairéad Donnellan

THE SYRIAN VIOLIN MAKER

After the voyage
he needed a home for the soul,
an instrument that might sing
of his history.
Aged maple was a gift
as were the tools he used
to carve out the body,
making a place to cradle survivors
whose names are written inside.

Beneath the veneer there is a space
aching for the gentle stroke of a bow
to coax out the chanting of children,
sunbirds, humming jasmine,
the drone of scooters in the street.
Yes, there is an elegy for all this,
the slow sawing of a life divided,
the frenzied tempo of a father's heart,
breast beating, wailing, sirens
rising to a crescendo
until there is nothing
but the welcome resonance
of waves breaking
on another shore.

Doreen Duffy

IN SEPIA

I killed my mother,
slowly.
Her smile died first,
the black and white image
more vivid
as she faded,
her laugh almost remembered
bubbled up in her throat
choking her words
until silence filled her, day
after day.
But at night she sang
notes to my father
before I was born,
when she had a life
and probably,
love.

Micheline Egan

PASSING THROUGH

I lined your coffin
with the *RTÉ Guide*
and some hand-made chocolates,
just in case you'd
be caught between worlds.

You, after all, thought
that the non-dairy diet
as specified by your heart man
didn't include your daily glass of milk
or your bar of Cadburys.

I wondered who'd be there
to meet you, to let you in.
Would you bump into Nehru, Gandhi, de Valera?
Or would you just keep in
with your own people?

Attracta Fahy

VISITING MANRESA HOUSE, SALTHILL

Six years old and visiting grandaunts,
her mother hired a hackney to get there.

Mary Ellen already waiting in the parlour, staring
at the Sacred Heart picture; a fire, china cups
painted with pink roses.

Delia took her to the sloping garden,
a clearing of yellowish grit, sand, the sea ebbing
burbling white foam almost at her feet.

Two arms stretch either side of the blue
ocean, short of embrace –
seaweed, salty air, a westerly breeze.

'They are pushing the sea
back to build a road.' Delia, leaving her to go inside.

Waves over rocks, her ears pumped
to its loud roar, the mewing of gulls,

hearing distant whispers, women
reading tea leaves, muttering about seeing a priest.

First time in a city, first time looking upon the sea.
Mary Ellen laid to rest months later
in the graveyard behind the house.

Carole Farnan

LADY SINGS THE BLUES

black-stemmed flower blooming at the mic stand
trademark white gardenia in your hair
sassy, confident, fronting a pale-skinned band

rooted in the rhythm, seeding sweet notes in the air
of a nightclub, heavy with smoke and sweat and beer,
holding them all in your palm as you tear

the ballad from your heart, each word an unshed tear,
surrendering its sad nectar, oozing heartbreak,
making it intimate, obscenely near

they come for you, Lady Day, to hear you take
a lyric, slur almost over the edge of a line,
almost falling, reaching for the ache

in later years the poppy's slave, unable to decline,
voice faltering, strange fruit decaying on the vine

Orla Fay

THE READER FINDS THE WRITER LOST IN THE WOODS

Halfway between real and imagined,
these shire roads are quiet,
save for birds chirping and warbling,
and robin redbreast is cheerful to sight,
chest ablaze like haws and Johnny McGoreys.

In the distance a muffled calling of voices,
children at play in the Elvish kingdom.
Already treetops shimmer in the vale,
in splendid hues of autumn, copper,
silver and gold, bronze, tin, and mustard.

This path becomes less worn and grassy.
An archway among trees is veiled,
visible only on close approach.
Two of the Sindar keep guard,
sentinels I greet who make no reply.

I am the reader of the poem. Outside,
but engaged. The entrant. A baton carrier.
Another candle flame whispering in the wind.
A follower of the trail. A thought on the river.
A shifting of energy, an idea ordained.

Viviana Fiorentino

CLEARING OUT
for my mother

We spent a whole morning clearing out the house,
kneeling in front of drawers left open,
clothes, books, souvenirs that we had forgotten,
hesitant on what to give, keep, throw away.

I fancied I could collect all
our lives yet enclosed in a myriad of objects,
like a nomad in the highlands of central Asia
busy with packing before leaving.

You leaned tiredly on a pile of old trousers
– maybe you wanted to hide under the throwaways
like in a den waiting
for the love of the living to return.

I would have liked to tell this story
as one of those of the ancient Latin people,
the naked truth of facts without adjectives
as if preparing for a new morning is just like making coffee

patiently pressing the dust into the filter.
At the end it's easy to dismantle.
Despite the resistance to preserve,
our species crumbles through centuries.

When we finished the clearing out,
we waited for the evening, one step after the light
in an almost empty house,
a minimum moment of being close

and then lost.

Amy Gaffney

SETTING TIME

The road doesn't know we're here
in the low end of the field;
behind the manicured hedges that
border
the woods and
the places where
the foxes cross the stream;
the ditches drip,
damp dew,
sticky
beechnuts pop, like
chicken bones under foot.
We are silently disruptive –
sending curled vibrations into the ferns.
Robins flit by; chirp-chirp-chirping to me
that I am
perilously close to a
boundary – a ditch, and a crusted metal thorn-ed wire.

Not one to sit on.

I almost speak aloud.
You almost hear me say
how glad I am now
that the marbled skies are lighter, and
the long winter days are more
bearable,
that time has a purpose, and how
you, turning the key every evening,
wind the clock within me.

Susanna Galbraith

it gets everywhere

the back of my hands waiting on my thighs
like pebbles or astronauts.

from the chair across the room from yours
I've caught myself

wondering how often you think about my bones
inside this long activity of loving.

from the corners of our eyes we've been watching it settle
from verb to noun

like something come inside from the weather –
this love like sand.

and when I open my mouth again I'm telling you how
much I want to swim when it rains

Sonya Gildea

THE WINDHOVER

Eighty on 40 West, 75 North, window down
crossing state lines – how many? three? four?
her child hand raised flat to breeze; lit, in flight
pressing sundrops between thumb and fingertip

cars overtake on both sides in whoosh and erase
she plays winter light over the back of her hand
turns it soft to her palm, eyes closed
a car passes, and another

he drives, more relaxed
her hand rises flat to county air; upright, held
– a standing bird, hovering in place
the underswish of wind

of wheels
speeding a Kentucky blacktop
she L-shapes her thumb, allows it stretch and reach
and perfect line

before folding it clearly across her palm
closing a small tunnel of fingers down and over
down and over, in sky, in hope
in coded TikTok signal

she repeats till evening
a gold wash on her skin
both lanes around them thin of cars
her bird hand hovers

until someone sees
until someone sees

Shauna Gilligan

1922

Capture –
put to memory
the sign of broken weather in the screech of the curlew;
that moment when you saw them coming;
how a cigarette filled wasted space,
between forefinger and thumb.

Captured –
let your body feel
the air by Massey's field, a last breath of freedom;
the *cuileoga* swarming, foretelling the heat;
how the cattle flicked their tails
filled you with such annoyance.

Captive –
realise, recognise
that turning you in was easier than speaking out;
the glass reflecting life outside, on the inside;
how beauty and brutality still fit
so tightly beneath your skin.

Anita Gracey

The Runt of the Litter

Born the year of the pig
in nineteen seventy one
between decimal day
and internment
squealing the element of metal
to streets of snipers
saracens and nail bombs
wolves danced at Lughnasa
in Belfast they howled.

I was more rage than girl
as the streets squealed fire
stone skimming in calm waters
I smell the plop of it on skull
disappearing into scribbled flaxen hair
the boy's divorced legs melted
raspberry syrup oozes.
Hoisting him like a white flag
they retreat to the barricades.
Thunderous backslaps erupt;
as stone echoes I take a bow
tempered by spilt metallic blood
I trot across broken glass.

It's the year of the determined ox
in twenty twenty one
hospital staff called to arms
under curfew again
I tilt my head sideways
to grasp the moon
pot belly bulges
rolling over I grunt quietly
as I root in the tangle of your chest.

Angela Graham

Archaeology, Llangorse Lake, Powys

I hold The Book of Excavations.
A crannóg, drowned, waited a thousand years
for someone to arrive whose eyes could see
and also read the seen;
whose heart leapt
to reach in, raise up, retrieve;
whose whole discipleship had readied him
to bring the comrades
who would read the treewright's alphabet
of *cleave, rive, rend,* of *mortise* and *augur-hole,*
decipher the embroiderer's silt-sodden script
and the songs in the spoil-heap of forgotten feasts.

The drawings, then, the meticulous notations,
the marquetry of find and speculation
till the place is known, and what remains unknown
fascinates.
I hold The Book of Excavations.
I hold a kind of love.

Mim Greene

RIDING THE TIGER

It's like a volcano, or a fist reaching up
through the centre of my body,
punching, flailing, vicious, out of control.
It's like a Bengal tiger pacing up and down,
stalking its prey. It's deep in my veins,
in my cells, for all the women in my line,
that have been held down, forced,
humiliated, not believed. It's the rage of ages.

It lets me know I have survived,
in fact I have thrived. Despite the odds,
against the odds, perhaps because of the odds.
The little girl who could not eat,
has a savage inside her that would devour worlds,
a 'No' so loud it shatters crystal.
This is her inheritance.

The voice of a million women standing firm behind her
shouting, bellowing, demanding, resounding ...
no more, no fucking more!
This is the power I contain,
restrain, repress, lock down, hide, submit ...
and I am off again.

So this time I turn and face my power.
I claim this forever as my own,
I climb on the back of that tiger,
no saddle, flesh on fur.
I rise to my destiny. No shame,
no shame. No more,
no more, I will let my anger roar.

Christine Hammond

SANDEEL BAY

Plaintive, the curlews sing
grey seals turn at the rocks
and my basket is replete
with sea-sprayed berries.

Later, bounteous
with black-purple jam
you declare it a perfect day
saying I made it so.

Storing jars, I realise
preserving is more than fruit.

Rachel Handley

In my dream you were alive. I said I
loved you and you heard me. You knew it was
me, not just distance with a human shape.
You tell me I need to stay here, so I
do. I grab the thread of sewn pink petals
hanging tight between us, their wet edges
drip your soft thunder all over the floor,
liquid velvet slips between our fingers,
soaked; we campaign to walk against time. Come
see me, you said, before I forget. You
knew, before we knew, that the dementia
was slithering in, knocking out pieces
of you with its blunt mouth. I'd put you back
together if I could, click each petal
into its stem so that I could say I
love you and you could hear me.

Niamh Hehir

THE ONION DRESS

I was a princess once, briefly unveiled;
the pea that gave it all away
was sharp despite the cushions,
felt as only one such as she could feel.
And yesterday I might have been a siren,
but for the cold casual bareness
she must carry with her always.
I cast that cloth away
and sought more substantial ground below.
Wrapping myself in darkness, a funereal bride,
rich with sober musings,
heavy with a queen like pride.
I ride wild camouflages,
speaking with a hybrid sound,
sweeping minor creatures from my path,
in the deep floods of my passing,
oblivious to it all.

To undress a woman is a difficult thing,
such a maze of pins, clips and stitches,
scraping layers away, searching for a single stretch of skin.
So easily deceived as each new layer
is so effortlessly conceived.
This is a canvas, too cluttered with imaginings
to be left bare, a cloak of oddly matched confusion,
breathing out images like busy eyes.
One I may borrow,
but never own.

Phyl Herbert

ODE TO PLEASURE

Deep in – it's all blackness.
Don't know how long I've been here
but I feel an urge to move upwards.
There's something pulling me and
I feel the light tickling my skin.

The sky and sun heat my innards.
I'm above ground breathing in the heat.
My pores open into flower,
I grow and grow and my roots
swell and swell and burst the bed
around my body.

I'm transported and laid on a table
peeled of my outer skin for the
transition of another miracle
losing myself into another's existence.

Nora Hughes

SPEECH SOUNDS REACH ME FROM THE GRAVEL PATH

Glides, clicks, plosives, gutturals
launch themselves over the waterway that lines
this urban marsh, over unruly
grass and vetch that burrows

through reedbeds, over baked walkways, past
the lonely blue of the boathouse,
blemish among the trees,
into the threads of green algae combed

through water by the synchronised pulling
and straining of the rowers.
Word-streams, like and unlike my own
outpourings and withholdings

in tongues like and unlike my own,
pass through me, their meanings sensed
or not: these strangers, fellow-talkers
have settled here, as I have, till our words

people the parklands. Something almost
like kinship can be sensed among
us and the ruminating cattle
brought to the marshes to crop and tame

the grass, their broad, striped backs
loved and loved again
as we pause our talk to hear
a low sound: grass blades ripping

from the ground, to be
chewed, liquidised and ruminated on.

Seanín Hughes

Voluntary Motherhood
reason for committal: medicine to prevent conception

'This is my body which is [broken] for you.'
– 1 Corinthians 11:23–25

And what of Mary's body breaking?
Her transubstantiation?
Holy Spirit twitched its nose and she became a blue egg –
egg the complexion of sky, skewed sphere of divinity, flesh
thin as shell when it cracked with a crowned head. She
was a child
softer than fontanelle, and not designed
to calcify.

We've always attempted ways and means,
trial and error: honeyed the mouths of our wombs,
gummed up plugs.
We became botanists, up to our crotches in silphium,
pennyroyal and Queen Anne's lace. Sounds deceptively
pretty on the tongue, yes?
– delicate camouflage in a quiet revolt.
I'll confess

to reading *Fruits of Philosophy* and knowing how
to keep my intimacies
a pinker shade of pure, flushed with blood and want.
A human colour.
I have no taste for chastity, bland and blinded to touch. My
body
need not split for the knowledge of another,
will not stretch to hold
more than I permit. It is mine,
it is mine, it is *mine*.

Linda Ibbotson

REFUGEE

The morning tasted of flambéed apricots
and discontent, as I unfold
a flotilla of paper boats
cut out from the shape of bones.
I take my brush, paint war and erase,
decide to paint a dove
to cover cracks in the sea.
In the distance
I saw a Nomad thread the world
through a hole in the sky,
place a mirror at his throat
to reflect the source of all things.
He read the palms of bone black statues
whose names I do not know,
hung the words
in the mouths of sea birds to dry.

Jean James

BEARING WITNESS

Dear Daughter,

The process of parting is already begun
as the midwife sweeps your undercarriage
with her right-angled mirror,
like the soldiers in Belfast,
nineteen seventies, checking cars
for explosives below.

Your knuckles bulge on the edge of the birthing pool
as you search for position.
Squat? Kneel?
Water ripples with pain; it pinks, like you.
Throes pass and come again.

Thirty-seven degrees of liquid temptation
before the air will hit.
A head appears and everything pauses.
You look serene but you've been
breached.

Your baby does not float;
no air on skin or in her lungs to cast her out,
instead she stays, anchored to her cord
until the next wave crashes,
launching her up and out,
onto your mothership.

And then you smile: miraculum.

Rosemary Jenkinson

SANDY ROW RIOTS

A long, hot summer is promised
in haw red letters daubed
on the baked outer wall

of inner city rath and bawn.
Enfurnaced people, copter-crazy,
entranced by gauzy wraiths

from flaming underbellies of engines
that catch like fireweed,
come from the east and Tiger's Bay.

Fireworks scythe the tarmac,
glow-flies bumping over peaty waters.
'They keep your feet warm!' goes the crack.

Saracens are lured into the crucible
of cul-de-sacs and, bombed,
reverse with rolling wakes of fire.

Rubble-cairns tipped from crates
are fed upon like bread for crows
and the leaders, snooded and scarfed

from mountain winds, orchestrate,
raking out old, dead fires for folk
on the brink of ceasefire suicide,

like drovers herding over gullies
where each year the heather is lit and burnt
so that it can live once more.

Nandi Jola

PICTURES OF THE PLACE

I used to wait on the edge of the window
each day for my child to come flying down the road,
her face filled in with a smile and the promise of things
to come.
The days were longer then.
The summers when there were kids everywhere,
the neighbours kept their doors open and the calls to
come play were constant.
Bring back those days of cartoons on the telly,
alphabet potatoes and dilute juice,
ice pops and curley crisps,
where chicken nuggets and chips were golden
and 10p mixup were a treat.
Bring back the milkman,
the sound of the ice cream van,
the sound of children playing in the fields,
trees where the birds perched and returned each year.
Bring back my dreams of the things that never were
and those flowers that never came back.

Nithy Kasa

MY PEOPLE DANCE BY THEIR HIPS

They let me in rivers
when I could stand above the ripples on my own,
the hidden bend for women,
beating clothes against the river banks,
that is where I heard about it
– waist beads, how men love
these things around women.
But we bought our beads for ourselves,
the people where I am from
dance by their hips,
with bead chains, leopard prints
wrapped on, you swirl to drums.
It's tradition. But women's talks in chambers,
almost to a whisper, were safe,
to stop pretending that you've never been touched,
and tell that you let him,
spell a poem on you, bare hands.
We shared tricks, recipes,
shea butter for the lines on your tights,
the sorcery you'll need to keep a fussy man,
and waist beads – men love
these things around women.
But we bought ours for ourselves,
the people where I am from
dance by their hips. It's tradition.
Our beauty pavilions have weeping willows
of bead bonds swaying, mirrors, brave to show
the days we used to wear skirts
above our knees have passed,
like rosary beads on a praying hand.
Still, I keep the beads around my hips,
the people where I am from
dance by their hips.

Virginia Keane Brownlow

LOBSTER RITUALS

On some childhood summer evenings, my mother
forgot her overdraft at the AIB Lismore, bought lobsters
from boats by the pier for seven and six a pound,
made garlic mayonnaise in a blue bowl with a wooden
spoon, smashed red lobster shells with hammers.

We reverently chewed muscular lobster bodies,
licked the insides of shells, poked skewers into claws,
picked out soft pink and white flesh. Swallowed slowly
as if we'd never taste another lobster, heads bent over
plates, respectful of her ritualistic homage to fish,
fishermen and feasting.

Wilma Kenny

WE COULD HAVE CALLED TIME

She hid for a while
lady bird in long tresses
long green grasses.
We brought gifts of violet
and raspberry claret;
white flowers and scarlet
berries scavenged from a nearby hedge.
She did not heal.

Time has moved us on; never to be turned.
Slow and easy she returned to us in her own way.
The scar hidden deep and low on her belly.
It is the hole he punched in the wall I will not forget.
That is when she called time.

Therese Kieran

ABOVE AND BELOW THE SURFACE
Belgian refugees, Monaghan, 1915

Young women bunch around the table,
its dark brown transformed to a blank canvas,
and like falling snow, a hush descends.

The women pierce and pull through hoops,
threads swim up, dive down,
the open sash becomes a radio,

plays magpie chatter, raucous crow,
buzz by bee, a braying donkey,
footsteps traipsing the yard, scraping.

You might be forgiven for thinking
they were praying, hearing only small pops
from zipped lips releasing pins

to the hem of the stitchwort gown,
while random satin stitches made petals
on quiet, unassuming whitework sewn by

quiet, unassuming women, until their feet
remember a dance, take up with an incoming whistle,
drift back to the colour of their past –

the crimson silk lining of a full-length fur,
gilt edge gold in the Royal Museum,
turret snipped roofs against a blue rinsed sky,

their Belgian home in hibernation,
waiting under white dust covers,
hearing their prayers worn to pearl.

Alice Kinsella

Sylvia Plath is Sitting in My Father's Chair

the red leather one by the fire. She's spinning
a wedding ring on a pen, dips it into the heat.
Her teeth glint like silkworms, her eyes like smoke.
She rubs her face with her hands, peels off a layer of skin,
blows it into the embers like ash in reverse.

I go to the bathroom, brush my teeth till they bleed.
She follows me and turns on the shower.
You know it's not going away,
she tells me as she steps in, fully clothed.
I haven't put on the immersion.
That's ok, I like it cold. I perch on the sink and smoke.
She uses my soap but it won't lather.

She leaves water all over my floor,
shakes out her hair like flames.
Can I get you a drink? No. I have something cooking.
I follow her through my own house.
She kneels by the hearth like she's praying.
Her hands don't burn, steam rises from them like clouds.
The wedding ring glows,
it slides down her tongue into black.

When I get up, she's cooking me fat white American eggs.
You look old in the mornings, she tells me,
like life is swelling under your skin.
That's just fat, and the cigarettes.
Are you going to write today,
about something other than the dead?
Fuck off.
It's miles from my house to the road.
She leaves barefoot, and I do not follow.

Susan Knight

AFTER THE READING

A short pale guy accosts the writers
one by one. Asks: How can I get published?
We wish we knew, we smile, mutter
words of encouragement. Try to slide away.

He fixes me with a lugubrious eye. I'm a softie
and anyway no one else is talking to me right now.
What is it? I ask. Fifty thousand words, he says.
I suspect they're all in that large brown envelope
clutched under his arm.
One word and he'll hand it over.
I say nothing.

It's a comedy drama, he adds (you'd better believe it).
He also does the rounds
of the clubs, making people laugh.
That's good, I say. He smiles bitterly,
his jokes are evidently no laughing matter.

I suggest a publisher I have a grudge against.
I sent it there already, he tells me. Got it back.
Sent it lots of places. I don't think they even read it.

I notice suddenly he has a swollen waist,
although he isn't fat.
Perhaps he's got a bomb strapped around himself.
Publish me or I'll blow us all up,
Roddy bleeding Doyle and all, he'll shortly shout.
Out of hand, over the edge.

We don't invite him
to join us later for a drink.

Jackie Lynam

SILENCED

I'm naked from the waist down
when they arrive;
a cavalry of white coats,
baby-faced, blank stares.

Incapable of summoning words,
my tongue ripped out by medical artillery
– it's been thirty hours since my waters broke.

The birth plan's flung to the ether:
a no man's land of paper wishes,
compiled by anxious women
in the dead of the night
when heartburn's scraping sleep from bones.

The midwife shoves a gloved finger
deep inside me.
1–2cm dilated.
Stoic and silent until midday,
when water and bile are violently expelled
and any pretence of being in control
evaporates.

A week later
the bill for the failed anaesthetic arrives.
Put up. Shut up. Pay up.

No plans conceived for
second and third labours.
I'm not the captain of this army.

Carmel Lynch

The Landing

The landing is empty now where once your fat legs
shuffled in heavy nappies to the refuge
of the pillows in our warm room.
The echo is long gone now of football boots
bounding down each day to play in the burning sun.
That space is silent now where steps once creaked
and young girls shrieked on tottering heels
as they crept into your private den of fun.
The secrets of the stairs are locked forever
into the dancing shadows of your past.
They had fled too soon before we even knew those
conversations couldn't last.
Your room leading from the landing now gapes
open with abandon.
The cluttered floor of yore swept clean of all
your mess.
The safe haven where you ran to blank the voices
droning on now has an eerie sound I can't embrace.
The door swings open widely,
no need to close it tightly anymore,
to say you're safely home from where you were.
No codes can reassure us now that you are curled
up close,
not lost out there in places we will never know.
You could be anywhere just now,
all certainties are gone.
And the door that once stayed open
as we smothered you with kisses
is closed firmly. The landing light is turned off.

Noelle Lynskey

THE CUT

In the solitude of the summer garden
a kindful peace drops, peering over the poppies,
the fuchsia, wafting on the paths
where a week ago my daughter, in a pink flowing
dress blended her mix of seed with soil,
sprinkling water on bud and clay; the promise
of blossoms in her parting smile, hugs
postponed until this all ends, her hair a halo
of curly waves, reminiscent of her childhood look
when the war between mother and girl saw her kick
the clay, stomp over any fresh buds, throw
water on the notion of cutting her long mane
of unbrushable knots that hid her eyes, her
face, her pubescent breasts, seedlings
of this woman who now garnishes my salads
with peppery rocket and little gems of May.

A scent of her lives in the notch of my neck –
her teenage peace offering one Mother's Day,
a locket laced with her curls, cut a decade ago,
a souvenir of the battles we choose,
the hurts we save for self, unspoken
words furled in our throats.

Her locks will be cut when the salons reopen.
She'll select her own style and shape,
WhatsApp a shot of her face, reframed.
No matter, I'll wave my white flag of approval,
battle lines long overgrown.
She owns her hair.

Colette McAndrew

THE WITNESS

On the most contested ground on earth,
praying you weren't the oldest,
hoping your legs and feet would hold up
and you wouldn't be more trouble than your worth.
No need to worry, no grounds for concern,
in the global brigade of helpers
bringing home the harvest.
Fat panting Americans perched on ladders,
leaning in among olive branches,
pulling purple fruit with sweat smeared faces,
oxygen tanks lolling at the roots of trees
planted in old god's time.

Hoping for a posting in busy downtown Jerusalem,
but billeted with shepherds in the Hebron valley.
Escorting schoolgirls through manned checkpoints
on their way to nowhere,
searched by soldiers
getting a grounding in violation.
Bearing witness to the humiliation of a people
holding on for dear life.
Watching footie and Sky News together,
as rockets leave their traces across the constellations.

Catherine McCabe

ORCA MOTHER

The grieving orca carries her dead calf for miles,
days, delicately balanced on her nose.
It isn't heavy
or an ordeal
for these mothers who will starve
while supporting their precious cargo
aloft, atop the perilous sea,
its powerful waves threatening to take twice
what has already left this world.

And isn't grief strange?
The way realisation of loss weighs heavier
than the dead carcass of a little one,
so loved.

Mary McCarthy

AT SUNRISE

When the roar of the world
is against you,
settle your rattled mind
by going for a walk on the road
like you own it.

Draw from the hills and valleys,
stillness that enraptures.
Watch for breaking light of the sun,
let your eyes drink in the wheat fields,
bear witness to vanished hands
that saved a golden harvest.
Relish this imprint of memory from long ago.
This could be harder.

Cluck like a chicken in the farmyard.
Now lightning charges in the sky,
now thunder clatters louder than breaking plates,
now an eerie silence.
Anything is possible at sunrise.

Helen McClements

Before She Went Down to the Grand Canal
RIP Ashling Murphy

I wonder if she chanced to run early,
catching the last of the waning sun
before darkness fell,
snuffing out the light.

I wonder if she felt proud,
proud that rather than go home, head full of chattering
voices, jotters to mark and spreadsheets to fill, and lounge
on the sofa until it all settled,

that instead,
she swapped her skirt for leggings,
her shoes for sneakers,
and set out,
breathing deep the cold, clean air,
and ran.

I wonder if she chose
the path she knew:
the trodden path, the busy path,
the path that any *sensible* girl would take,
when *being so bold as to run alone.*

I wonder if she knows that we hold her close,
in Belfast, in Derry, in Dublin, in Cork:
that yesterday, as a breeze blew in from the east
that the candles we lit flickered, then faltered but
kept
on
burning,
just as her light will continue to do.

Ellie Rose McKee

IS IT PROBLEMATIC TO THINK MY MUSE
MIGHT HAVE ADHD?

I pick up a pen
    and my fingers itch for a paintbrush

I get out my paints
    and start to wonder to what I should listen
    or watch
    or read

I read a book
    or start
    and get two sentences in
    and get a story idea
    a poem idea
    a screenplay pitch
    and a tweet, in entirety

I pick up a pen ...

Maeve McKenna

YOUR MOTHER, FOR YEARS

When you recall your mother's
unravelling, you don't speak
of her waist-length black hair
tangled in an elastic band,
occasionally released like a swarm

of flies across the table oilcloth.
You don't say her hands frantically
swatted the braids – pasty fingers
surfacing like maggots
through muck.

Once, you caught sight of a knuckle,
and for months after denied
you dreamt it was a tooth
from the only dog your father homed
and starved, buried

by then under the Chestnut tree
in the back yard, roots that crept upwards,
forcing foundations on the scullery floor,
glass milk bottles perilous
at a tilt. She never moved from that chair,

you fail to say, except sometimes to sit
at the sewing machine, the needle's eye
unthreaded, one foot motionless
on the waxed linoleum, the other tapping
and tapping the missing treadle.

Triona McMorrow

EMPTY

Rotted curtains in ribbons,
hiding nothing, a house in ruins.

Black-faced sheep and old baths
in fields under the stars.

Half-restored cottages abandoned
yet again, emigrants return.

A load of breeze blocks delivered
to someone who held the dream.

The footprints of cattle in the kitchen,
because nobody closed the door.

Josepha Madigan

(*from*) ON A BREAK UP

You are angry
at yourself
for letting him
control you,
mould you
into something
you are not,
nor ever
will be.
You cannot
cage
a lioness,
you feel like
shouting
at him,
yet you don't.
You are still
desperate
for him
at this point.
You tell him
no one
is ever
to call him
Squishy,
that you'll
love him
forever
no matter what.
Please stay,
your heart screams.
He doesn't
hear it.

Katie Martin

HALLOWEEN BALL

They went to the ball,
the bastard daughters

of Sir William Wilde,
costumed in the latest styles,

tutored for more than shadow lives.
The provincial well-to-do in awe

of their exquisite steps,
fine silhouettes.

They lingered in a room
not made for dancing.

A spark caught Mary's crinoline.
Emily, quick to her aid, became a flame.

For a flash, Isola was reborn,
the glowing child, the ray of light.

Rolled in the snow, too late,
the ugly sisters now. They suffered

on for days. The record states
'Wylie' was their name.

Orla Martin

ANDROMEDA

We should have gone to Andromeda, to visit my cousins
even though they live in a dimension where everything
is upside down
or made of fish
or whatever laws of physics are in vogue at the time,
should time exist.

Andromeda. Stellar cities of red stars and shiny new
blue ones.
A super supercluster!
Oh, we could have had fun at the Pinwheel. Trips to
the Triangulum.
Quasar shows.
Centaurus A being closed, due to star bursts.

Two trillion galaxies in this finite yet unbound universe
and you take me to this heliocentric cul-de-sac.
'Failed star with old storm. Too much dark matter.
Primordial at best', according to *Galaxy Advisor*.
'Pale Blue Dot ok. Could not get tickets for Radiohead. Not
worth a Drake Equation.'
'Down with sizeism! Solidarity for Pluto!'

Did we just pass the junction for the Heliosphere again?
I told you to take a left at the Kuiper belt.
They call it the Zone of Avoidance for a reason!
We'll end up stuck on that fossil Sedna. *Welcome to Sedna,
we have methane!*
I told you, we should have gone to Andromeda.

Jennifer Matthews

SELKIE

You like to dance in the moonlight, barelegged.
You like to take stories into your body and rebirth them.
You like to press words into the pleasure of puzzles.

There's no dance unless Selkie slips out of her skin.
There is no performance without an audience to listen.
There's no collection without a spine & a recommendation.

The man on the beach who says he's your husband.
The man in the hotel room who says this is an audition.
The man with your drink who says he's your mentor.

Your skin in the hands of another.
Your skin in the hands of another.
Your skin in the hands of another.

No return home without your pelt to swim in.
No screen to perform on without his invitation.
No words to reply when he says yours are worthless.

She left home and undressed. This is what happens.
She followed him in the room where no one could see them.
She surrendered her words when she accepted a drink from him.

The submerged eyes in the ocean watching you naked.
The assistant outside the door, scheduling his next meeting.
The money handed over for each volume of poetry.

Your skin in the hands of another.
Your skin in the hands of another.
Your skin in the hands of another.

Mari Maxwell

TOO CLOSE FOR COMFORT

The stranger ran to you
by the Rosslare train line.

Hands in his pockets,
burrowing deep.

Collar up, covering up.
Our only child out of sight.

Terror in our guts, heartbeats spinning,
our steps stumble and rush.

There, around the corner, you
kneeling in the gravel.

He, veering direction, dashing
away over the bridge.

'I was searching for a rock
to hit him with,' you explain.
Our ten-year-old daughter
battle ready.

Anesu Khanya Mtowa

SOON, MY LOVE

I can't stop writing poems for the lover I have never met.
In one, the lover is spilling her shadow over my bed,
teasing the curtain with the flex of her toes
and asking me to kiss her in all the places the moon greets
her skin.
In my poems, the lover is all limbs,
all air-guitar fingers and overstretched calves.
The lover is written into lines pulled from the refraction of
boiling summer light, the lover is the modest sway
of wind chimes, the lover is the dizzy head
of a dandelion.
I wonder if the lover is waiting for me to free her
from the grasp of my breath. I have locked the lover
into a dozen forgotten notebooks. I have trapped her
as a thin layer over ballpoint steel.
The lover is written into every moment I have
ever longed to own.

So when I meet my lover, my real and living love,
I will not stop to write a thing. I will leave her be
to breathe
from beyond the page, rest
my idle poet hands on each corner of her flesh
and have her tell me everything she has ever known.
And if she asks, I will let her burn every word
I ever made her out to be.

Elizabeth Murtough

Sea Change

I shouldn't like to say, but really
I'd been waiting – wearing
the steady pull of sunlight
on my stem, leaning
toward the window of whatever

room I walked in. I was expecting
fire, an orange peel
of light, some incorrigible
combustion to turn
an ordinary sequence

into a sigil.

Instead, a fish
-shaped shadow

slipped itself from my throat,
sought the always-open skylight

and was gone. On the other side

of the street, a woman felt the fabric
soften as she dressed
her daughter, and the chimney's
uneven, corrugated metal siding
accepted heat and silvered.

Mitzie Murphy

THE GAG CLAUSE

*By the end of 2015, 15,579 women and men were paid a sum of
money to compensate for the suffering they had been put through in
industrial homes run by religious orders in Ireland. My mother
Mary was one of them.*

They tried to gag you.
Put hands over
your mouth
to stop you speaking.

Never come back.
Never ask for more money.
Never speak about it again.
It's a gag clause!

Sign it, they said.
Silence has its price.
Sixty six thousand.
You bought a new couch.

Paid off the credit union.
Put a shower in.
Gave the rest to family.
Nothing changed,

nothing at all.
Distant apologies
never reached your door.
Your stories

were a way to live this life.
They can never gag
a storyteller.
They will never gag me.

Úna Ní Cheallaigh

NOCTURNE

Sleep – you took it with you.
So many nights I've longed to close my eyes,
drift at last into dream. I do not blame

you for robbing me of rest, you have given
stillness – silent hours waiting
for day to slowly break through the skylight;

a welcome chorus of birdsong, drowned by gulls
screeching in flight as they leave the strand,
a foghorn beyond the lighthouse at Poolbeg

and your last dawn when the ice-moon
was on the verge of waning, a fox crossing
the hospice carpark its tail barely touching

bold white lettering on black tarmac
guiding you, marking your exit.

Éilís Ní Dhuibhne

WHO WANTS TO GO?

Margaret Mac Curtain died today.
I remember, I remember
when she was Sister Ben,
when the history students
in group nine (or ten?)
dropped her name
on the corridors of Belfield
like hankerchiefs or gauntlets.
Dudley, and someone else, and Sister Ben.
It was all about their names then,
who said hello to whom, did the professor nod to them?

Then she stopped wearing her habit
and became Margaret,
middle-aged and feminist.
The history students were scattered
to RTÉ, the Four Courts
and Dáil Éireann.
They were chauffeuring their kids
to school, and rugby, ballet lessons. Art.

Five years ago she said to me:
'Life gets hard after you are eighty.'
Pains and aches, and such things.
She was eighty six.

And yet
nobody really wants to go.

Ciara Ní É

TAOS FIACLA

Rith mé as taos fiacla inniu
ní raibh slaimice fágtha sa tiúb

chuardaigh mé gach cófra sa teach ach
níor aimsigh mé tada a dhéanfadh an jab

faoi bhrú, scríob mé mo scuab ar an ngallúnach láimhe
agus líonadh mo bhéal le sobal tiubh láidir
agus géarbhlas dodhearmadta

ceacht foghlamtha
níl aon ní ar aon dul le taos fiacla

nuair a scaramar, a chroí
chuardaigh mé ionadaí
ach drochbhlas a bhí orthu ar fad

ceacht foghlamtha
níl éinne ar aon dul leatsa

is trua nár thuig mé sin
sular rith mé as
sular rith mé as
sular rith mé

Ava Ní Loingsigh

Ag rith thart ag iarraidh gach rud a thaifeadadh,
is a thabhairt chun cuimhne, peann inár lámha againn,
tá rud deas faoi féachaint siar
ach is deacair an rud é a bheith ann is á dhéanamh sin,
tá línne ann táim cinnte ach níl sé infheicithe i gcónaí,
na rudaí a mbíonn cead againn
agus nach mbíonn cead againn scríobh fúthu,
camera agat le pictiúirí luí gréine beagnach
chomh hálainn is a bhí sé ag an am,
uaireanta bíonn sé níos fearr gan scríobh
faoi roinnt rudaí fiú dá mbeadh ort an fonn,
saol is ealaín ag teacht salach ar a chéile,
trína chéile, toirsiúnach,
is iontach an rud é an fhilíocht
ach ní bhíonn sí i gcónaí oiriúnach.

Gormfhlaith Ní Shíocháin Ní Bheoláin

Ispín Veigeatóra

Aréir taibhsíodh dom gurbh ispín mé
dubh dóite.
Mo chraiceann ag pléascadh
cloig ar gach orlach díom.
Saill ag sileadh amach mar dheora feola
laistigh de mo chulaith theann craicinn dhóite.
Bhí faid bhándearg chreimthe mhionfheola ionam
cothrom comhionann cumannach
le gach aon ispín eile.
De gheit a thuigeas gurbh fhuath liom feoilséantóirí
mar gur theastaigh uathu m'ispínteacht a ghoid uaim
gan trócaire.
Nuair a bhreac an solas trí chaipíní mo shúl
bhraitheas barróg cheana mo leannáin veigeatóra.

Denise Nagle

HOW TO DISAPPEAR

War helps,
serves to make you shrink,
to make things dwindle.

That space that is your house tightens
to a small square of attic or basement
where even light can't seek you out.

After an explosion
you wear your powdered past.
Silence is your new parlance.

Sea crossing teaches you
how quickly colour is brushed out
by relentless grey, or darkness,

or noise, like that gush
of rush hour's six lanes, where you
– marooned on a concrete island –

bow your head. In your hands,
a limp sign, *Famille Syrienne.*
I pass, look back from behind glass.

You're almost there.

Margaret Nohilly

A TIME FOR EVERYTHING

I watch you from the kitchen window
fasten twine to guide the drill you dig;

slide a lath along to smooth the ridge;
poke finger holes, arm's length apart:

dark funnels for the seed you scatter
from a packet in your pocket; sift clay

for finer cover; fist fertilizer pellets from
the yellow bowl I used to use for baking.

Through the wishbone of your thighs,
your back arched over, supple still,

I sense your core alignment amid
daffodils, warm sunshine, robin twitter;

as if I knew. Did even you suppose
this yearly planting ritual had run its course?

Helena Nolan

WHAT TO EXPECT WHEN YOU'RE PUNCTUATING

At night, when all the callers leave, you hide in poems,
admiring the egg and sperm of the semicolon;
that eager tail that never meets the spot until
the tiny tears of commas fall and drop, to scatter,
here and there, across the page, and then you come upon
the period. She looks a little larger than her relatives.
Then what can you do but smile to see a question
marking her quizzical shape in typical style – why?

She is something of a swollen exclamation, so
tell her all your sisters and all your brothers' wives
have fallen pregnant! Then watch her
dematerialise in tight 'quotation marks'. Now
say that the lives of children
are the lines of poems you are writing
on a womb-white page.

Margaret O'Brien

ON MAKING SAUERKRAUT FROM PURPLE CABBAGE
Sauerkraut, *chopped cabbage fermented in brine, a miracle,*
first brought to Europe by the nomadic Tartars

I pick up the largest knife
from the kitchen block
(at this work I need leverage)
and slice this purple beauty into quarters,
then into smaller and ever smaller slivers.
Beside me, a mound of crisp ribbons
rises up in the bowl.
It all begins to glisten
as I sprinkle in some sea salt
and mix it together with my hands –
little stars of salt cling to my skin.
I dip my index finger into the brine,
taste the saltiness,
savour the tang on my tongue.

Earlier, I had been for a swim in the sea.
In the brine I swim, in me it swims.

I spoon the ribbons into the crock,
weigh it down beneath the protective brine.
The alchemy soon starts in the salty dark –
the transformation is complex
but the conditions are simple,
as the microbes, the *lactobacillus,* do their work.

The days pass, then I begin to hear
the soft burping sounds
of fermentation and I also hear from a far distance,
once upon a time,
a baby, drowsy on my shoulder.
The little miracles.

Harriet O'Carroll

ABOUT THE BABIES

About the babies lining the cupboards,
stacked in the storehouses,
heaped in the garden.
Job lots, special offers, luxury items,
begotten by their only begetters.
Man proposes.
The General begat some babies,
as did the politician, carpenter, powerbroker,
pop-singing playboy.
Babies to be allocated.
Stockman Daddy.
Hangman Pa.
Ploughman Parent.
Patriarch.
Lawman.
Babbikins
lying about and dying,
needing attention.
But the boat is burning,
armies massing,
and the thing he has his eye on imbibing
more than his slice of the cake.
Babies growing unavoidably
into a mess of flesh for Daddy's army.

Sarah O'Connor

AIRPLANE LULLABY

I screened through four ebooks
on early pregnancy loss
staving off the awful hunch
persuading myself out of it

I read stats on miscarriage
inverting percentages
making figures work for me
by sheer will alone

my little love, you were the single stanza
I had housed for us both
oh, how we had wanted
all your poetry to bloom

I sang the same snatch of melody
over and over
mangling Dylan's lyrics in my head
begging you to stay

how was I to know
you had already winged away

Grace O'Doherty

SIEGE

These are false weeks. The city flocks to empty spaces,
leaves its doors unlocked.
Balconies jut from buildings like open drawers,
their jungle mess of living hanging out.

You turn up in spring green, in heat,
push your heels into the damp grass of a crowded park.
Kids in black coats wait for sirens.
There are fires always somewhere in the city.

Margaret O'Driscoll

When You Get There

On the way to Santiago your skin and rucksack
will stretch as one, walk with stars, call the dawn.
Listen to the gentle alarm of the goat bells, inhale the scent
of wild thyme. Dig deep. That urge to walk one million
steps along an ancient way is a strange one, but walk
you must until you cannot lift one other step.

Challenge yourself. On the way, sing the songs
your mother sang as she toiled,
'keep right on to the end of the road,'
'keep punching till you make those punches tell,'
aloud so your toenails join in, roar them over and over,
watch notes escape from your hair,
'animo!' a weathered farmer shouts, 'keep going.'
And others you meet along the way, the same refrain,
when you get to Santiago, when you get to Santiago.

Even cows in fields cease the cud and the horses stare.
Stare again at the doctor as she shuffled the pages
that rearranged your life, white words, her mouth like
goldfish seen through glass. That old refrain.
Grasp tightly the strong stone in your pocket,
forged from mountains, polished by restless tides.
Continue across the red clay of Rioja, trudge the Meseta
and Paramo and wet ditches of Galicia.

Bone worn. Set out from O Pedrouzo on the last camino to
Santiago, when you get there, when you get there,
Santiago, Finisterra, the end of the world,
there is nowhere to go,
then there is nowhere left to go.

Orlagh O'Farrell

ON THE SIDE OF THE VOLCANO

You've been a bright slope, mother,
one of those bright dangerous slopes
where magma's never far from surfacing.

And you're still
bubbling away
somewhere under my surface.

I come through my own hall door
to a momentary ghost,
a quick mental pocket-check

as if I might be late for something
or should have tidied a room,
and I've put my things down

on the ceramic stovetop
before time flows forward again.
But it's a pact, isn't it,

when people live
on a volcano's smouldering side
they cultivate danger,

but glory in lemons, apricots, vines.
You have
one foot in the underworld now,

hardly ever returning,
whatever the season.
I like her exceedingly,

my father's diary said
on the night you met.
More than any, for aeons.

Lani O'Hanlon

IN THE TIME OF NO TOUCH
after 'Quarantine' by Eavan Boland

When hospital staff couldn't hold the hands
of the dying, and their families
were forbidden to see and touch them,

nurses filled plastic gloves with warm water,
placed one over and one under the dying person's hand,
to mimic the pressure, the warmth

of a living hand – the hand of God they called it.

You had to stay overnight in the hospital in Waterford.
The porter wheeling you through corridors said
'At night everyone can move freely

but during the day a hundred security guards.'

And the masked guards stopped us on the way
to and from the hospital. Where have you been?
Where are you going? Who did you touch?

I couldn't see their faces but their hands were bare.

I saw the photograph; the age-spotted hand,
like grandad's, my father's,
held by balloons shaped like hands.

In the time of no touch,
I held the ones I love
body to body, breath in breath, breast to breast.

Lianne O'Hara

YONI

Three deaths.
A tedious abjection – a mother
who fails to recognise her own.

I am stillborn,
a misconception
nursing outdated fixations:

I love you, etc.

to no avail,
I play with his bones, build
sandcastles from ashes;

my hands raw with want
and now, undressing me
with meticulous care,

you treasure your revenge:

what is this?
it is oddly shaped, its face
is too soft for a boy.

No, this is not mine.

Judy O'Kane

I sat, semi-conscious
in the safe house
on the outskirts
of the city.

Where are you
on life's journey?
asked the sisters.
No one wore a habit.

They said
will you have a glass
of chateau cardboard?
Hosted by a painter,

a prison chaplain
and a psychotherapist,
I continued south.
Books towered

on bedside tables
from Waiheke Island
to Invercargill.
I kept company

with Katherine
Mansfield. I sat cross-
legged,
head bowed,

Siofra O'Meara

from THE TANGLING

Truth is, I'll pick apart pores behind closed doors,
rubbing milk spills, up on all fours.
You're doing so much, but it's still not enough.
Over-sanitised hands make your skin rough.
Tough it out, you're almost there.
Still chewing bits of thinning-out hair.
Bare all for the world, without it asking,
no sense of self so I'll borrow yours.
Flakes of skin chip off, like old paint,
taint nice places through association,
of devastation, no explanation,
so it's silence you choose.
Keep biting your lips and you'll get a bruise.
Who's that you're talking to?
Just a friend.
Well, we're not friends.
But foot sinks deeper into melting sand,
a change from a dried-out land.
Fanned by brochures of getaways and trips,
tips on how to keep fit during a crisis,
prices have soared, and can't afford the help
when it can be spent on paying rent,
leant in to get a light for a smoke,
laugh at hostile comments – in the hope it's a joke,
choke on strands, caught in throat – note taken.
Knees shaking – and you must be mistaken
because I actually don't give a shit.
Tangled enough to lose your wit,
sit in a cool dry place,
and wait till you turn, curdled and stink,
then to be poured down the kitchen sink.

Ruth O'Shea

NATIVE TONGUE

Listen to the landscape you breathe into being
when you speak your native tongue.
Macha.
Bóinn.
Fóladh.
Mór Ríogáin.
Your vowels a rhythmic drum.

Listen to the wildness that sings through your skin
when you begin to form the words.
Grá.
Crógacht.
Áilleacht.
Láidreacht
of bark and wing and fur.

Listen
to the howls that surface.
Listen.

You are closer than you think.

Sarah Padden

Oscar Wilde's Mother's People

Here's a thing –
Oscar Wilde spent childhood summers
just up the road with his mother's people
in a house on the edge of Lough Corrib,
surrounded by old abbeys and castles
and near to a cairn located at the end
of a grass-fed lane that marks the battle
of Firbolgs against The Danaan, *fadó fadó*

and in the understated way of ancient places
it isn't swamped with tourists every autumn
carrying yellow books and canes whilst
reading aloud *The Ballad of Reading Gaol,*
a golf resort called Wilde's hasn't been built
in the grounds of their summer house,
the signpost pointing to his granny's grave

hasn't been erected, the churchyard doesn't
include a craft shop called 'Flynn's of Shrule'
but when you've been here long enough
someone will drop Oscar's mother into
the conversation, as though everyone knows
she's from here, sure why wouldn't you,
and in the aural way of ancient things
the story lives on ...

Saakshi Patel

BASHIRAN

Oh, how this woman waltzes in, alight
with the vim of triumphant parades:
her laugh a booming bass drum, loud and bright
in harmony with clarinets, gently played.
Braving scorching Delhi summer heat
for humble wages an old couple can spare,
she sings her way through washing clothes, sheets,
veggies, shelves, trinkets, porches, chairs.
Her purse jingles by the fall of dusk
but empties out as cheap illicit spirit
into her husband's liver, turning him brusque,
fuelling his habit, enraging mind and fist.
She saves remaining change for her son's bail,
prances to work, refills her purse the next day.

Janet Pierce

SACRED SPACE

full of anguish
I turn to you
in silence

an oasis –
a balm –
a resting
for my soul.

Ruth Quinlan

THE LIFE OF A SCHOLAR

It was a time when I smoked cigarettes like the French –
blew smoke as lassoes across the air
towards boys at bars who moved from pints of milk
to pints of stout as the evenings darkened,
drank their courage up before going hunting.

I wore jeans as armour and siren call, hung them
like tiger skins in my wardrobe, the spoils of war –
or rather hours of stalking thrift stores for a pelt,
the perfect lure to draw young warriors away
from Scylla and Charybdis on the dancefloor.

My nails were eagle talons, electric blue or poppy red,
grown to scratch my name in ogham on the line of a spine
– or stroke the leather of classic novels displayed
upon my shelves like mounted stags, trophies
of days and nights between their pages.

And my hair was dark as earth beneath a chestnut tree,
thick like rope and strong enough to bridle skittish men –
or lay as pillow beneath my head when rolling late at night
in German trams with nightclub queens who couldn't sleep,
too in love, like me, with their own magnificence.

Heather Richardson

HOMEWARDS

That tock you hear is the old world
tilting another notch towards midwinter.
By the time you step outdoors the sun's already set,
and the sky's a mermaid balayage.
Cold, you think, but it's not.
Not as cold as it should be.

The last of the schoolchildren trudge from the bus
uniformed in mourning. They pass you,
eyes averted, ears blocked shut.
Your heart says to them,
'You will be old one day, please God.'

And just like that you are back
to another winter afternoon, crushed
in the backseat fug of your lift home from school,
a tangle of woolly tights and stomach cramps.

Your mother hangs her coat up.
The central heating ticks the house to life.
The pan hisses on the stovetop. That kitchen colour
scheme – orange and avocado.
What were the 70s thinking?
The evening yawns between *Scene Around Six*
and *News at Ten*.
You play one record over and over again in the lounge,
or read that poet out loud to yourself in your bedroom,
your schoolbag slouched in the corner,
and you wonder when
when
when
will your life begin.

Mary Ringland

PEEL

A woman took a vegetable knife
and with devotion began to cut the skin
of an apple, round and round in one long
tail until it collapsed, a perfect empty coil,

a shed skin. People she could do without
sprang to mind, and she pictured kneading
them with warm hands until they formed a ball.
Then with one closed fist she pressed down

to mould a swallow cup. Next she took fear,
imagined it as something she could roll
beneath straight fingers until it was slight.
In her mind's eye she tipped it in to fill the gap.

Now the cup was full but the shape was flat.
She had felt the threads of shame, secrets
and regret weave themselves into her years,
she found their ends and tugged until

they snapped. She would tie the strands
and make a plait. She could see it fold easily
into a dome-shaped heap. The ball complete,
she smeared it with doubt, it would stain her fingers

but bind the matter. She conjured up the pale flesh
she had formed, saw herself curl the peel from the top
round and round, carry it outside and set it on the lawn,
for worms to burrow and blackbirds to pierce.

Natalie Robinson

DAYDREAM

Lie perfectly still on a perfectly-made bed,
stripped down to nothing at all.
Levitate –
you are not in your body.

Mechanical birds call you from the sun.
There are tens of thousands of them.

You are alarmed as you wake,
how fast and shuddering it feels,
how dizzying.
Remembering that you are.

Your secrets fall from the windows into a courtyard
you don't have a key for.
Scattered, you cannot collect these parts of yourself.

Lie perfectly still on an unmade bed.

Mary Alacoque Ryan

The Last Word

Her dance is gone.
I see it in her body.
Slightly slower,
barely bent,
sadder.
No more dancing around the kitchen.
No matter what the music,
her song is gone.

The atmosphere thicker.
No need for words anymore.
Two hearts locked in rigid resignation.
'That's life', he said.
Always the last word.

Breda Spaight

Mother's Plum Pudding

Mix one pound each of jail-bait raisins
and #MeToo currants with finely chopped
patriarchy suet. Add a half teaspoon of
pornography nutmeg, two of pope's penis
allspice; one of glass ceiling cinnamon;
one cup of candied faking it, followed by
the grated rind of one ball-buster lemon.
A half cup of incompetent cervix brandy.

Soak one pound of female infanticide breadcrumbs
in one cup of sherry or foot binding. Combine
one dozen equal pay eggs, well beaten;
one cup of male gaze milk; one
and a half of zipless fuck sugar. Fold in
the dry mix, the bowl blonde at your breast.
Steam for aeons over fire fed on female flesh.
Let me know how you enjoyed it.

Eilis Stanley

A GRUMBLE FROM GAIA

I'm grieving the vanished act of looking.
I mean any kind of looking, looking up
or looking out and, at the risk of being wildly
outré, even a bit of looking at one another.
My train slides past Dalkey, round the horseshoe
of Vico Road. Inside, heads are bent and thumbs

all go. And now a bereft sky won't bother changing
hues anymore; depressed cumuli huddle in waiting
rooms and windless tunnels. Yesterday, the sun
threatened to stop casting shadows. As for throwing
silver over our glacial lakes, she's added that loss to her
list of absences. If only someone would take time

to see the gunmetal sea before she downs tools and stops
her ebb and flow altogether.
Not being noticed is the worst,
robin pouts, his breast a puff of crimson. I hear
the moon's having a special November bleed but apart
from some love-struck stars, she anticipates being alone
and saddest of all, unadmired. And we, furious, tender,
agile, old, keep missing being here
to forever be somewhere else.

Sarah Strong

THE DISLOCATED SHOULDER
in memory of Eithne Strong

There was a time
when my mother's arm
became peculiar and long,
hung like a dead thing
by her side.
She screamed in pain,
brought her left arm across
her chest to hold
the flattened place where
her shoulder should be –
a knob protruding now
where it should not be,
from beneath her collarbone.

I did not know what to do,
my hands flew forwards,
my hands flew backwards,
I pressed against the wall
to give her space.
My godfather, a bonesetter,
took my place.
His hands drew the limb
with gentle traction, returning
the slippage to its socket
with a click.
The doctor said her
rotator cuff muscles were lax,
taxed as she was with babies,
breast-feeding
and writing her poems.
She laughed at the name of
the troubled bone – *The Humerus.*

Lila Stuart

SKINS

Sometimes she feels
like an onion:
not a red one
vibrant and exotic
but more ordinary
than extraordinary,
a has-been one,
the runt of the bunch.

Her outer shim is akin
to crinkly paper,
brittle and dry –
no hint of smell
to well up tears
in anyone's eyes,
or extract flavour
to savour or
complement a dish.

Someday –
she'll sprout out,
nurturing her green
shoot of defiance,
rebelling against
the creeping dryness,
thirsting and bursting
through the dread,
her silent comfort
disturbed,
all her skins shed,
and her parched voice
heard.

Rosamund Taylor

EARTHLY PARADISE
After *Adam and Eve in their Earthly Paradise,*
Johann Wenzel Peter

I was disappointed by the Sistine Chapel.
There. I said it.

Priests sashayed to microphones
to intone, their voices echoing,
This is a sacred place. Be quiet.
It didn't feel sacred. Though winter,
it was close and hot, the crowd
jostling my ribs and hips. The ceiling
blurred: through binoculars,
the Sibyl's hand came into focus,
then her chest, like in a peepshow.
I was glad to escape to the corridor

and breathe. I almost fell into the Garden
of Eden. Colour poured from the frame
onto my sweaty face. Glasses
slipping down my nose, I saw
red monkeys, gold parrots.
A child's paradise of creatures:
fat guinea pigs nestled by serene sheep,
peacock paraded past pelican
and heron and turkey and lioness.
A camel eyed me and I hoped
she'd spit from her sensuous lips.
This was why I'd come here –
to be humbled, like Adam and Eve,
by the wealth of what I'd been given.

Csilla Toldy

CIRCE

The rocks roll. I was blinded by Ulysses' prostitution,
selling his body to me while lying about love only that
once .I believed. After a while you stop counting the men
you slept with. They are embedded in the texture, the
composition of the painting of your being, layer by layer
like a brush stroke – the tame lions and tigers licking your
hand, and perhaps at the bottom of each wrinkle there is a
lovemaking deep down, a little death. Scylla was a victim,
she did not know a thing – yeah – she was pretty and
desirable; she betrayed her country and her father for a
man – the true love of herself. Beauty is a self-offering,
seemingly innocent. But I, wise old Circe, know that her
beauty is a trap – like all these men I slept with – and
transformed into beasts. Now Scylla has to wear the girdle
of dogs and scare away any man approaching. When the
rocks roll she sinks their ships. I let Ulysses move on.

Jean Tuomey

We Speak in Flowers

My sister sends a purple allium,
the first flower our father drew for us,
its starburst spikes planted
in pencil on the page.

I reply with a foxglove, trust
she will remember the dress-up day
we wore their thimble blooms as jewellery.
I try to send a bee buzzing in the memory,
it will not pose.

I want to send her the open beauty
of my yellow rose – its peach perfume.
But its petals close for good.
I put it in the compost bin.
I only share good news.

Sometimes we speak in birds, her blackbird
in the birdbath before bedtime, my robin
scavenging every last crumb on the patio,
a final clear up once the sparrows have flown.
I settle on my thrush.
We both like its measled chest.

Every day we talk in mother.
My sister sends her reading in the shade,
weeding the bluebell patch from a chair,
or leaning over on her stick to greet
a long-awaited peony.

When there are no pictures,
I send a heart.

Molly Twomey

HEIRLOOMS

My dietician says if I don't eat,
my oestrogen won't restore.
My body will always be a door

locked on its hinges,
safeguarding its room
of dust and secrets.

Her son behind her scribbles
as if his life depends on it.
He is heavy enough that she could use him

as a kettlebell for Russian twists,
a dumbbell for deadlifts.
I shake my thoughts off,

ask if eating disorders are genetic.
If I will pass on this loss
of friends, bone mass, conscience.

Milena Williamson

CHARM FOR CATCHING A TRAIN

I buy a return and say she wants the same.
The man gives her an accidental discount,
a kind of love, and she fumbles with the coins.
Without touching, I show her what she needs,
and the exact change passes between our palms.
I take her by the elbow and through the gates
before we trade to-go cups to stir and wonder
how the vanilla is more aftertaste than taste.

This also might be love. At the end of the line,
we will find the castle and boats setting sail.
She asks how to alight, whether people
go one at a time or everyone alights together.
The platform number is days spent in love.
A train arrives from the right direction.

Pauline Bewick

visual poems